W9-AHJ-655

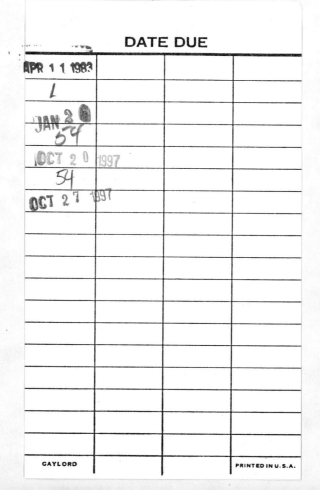

EX LIBRIS

abc
This is a book of letters &
defgh
writing &   people
ijklmn
speaking to one another, to themselves &
opqrs
to you, their   words   shaped by
tuvw
their   hands & by the history of
xyz
shapes

Letterbox
the art & history of letters

Jan Adkins
writing, illustration & design

Walker and Company, New York

ABCDEFGHIJKLMNOPQR

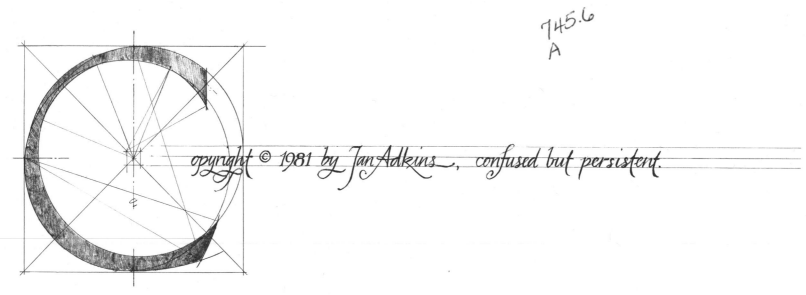

copyright © 1981 by Jan Adkins, confused but persistent.

745.6
A

Not so fast. Before you get into the book we have this little announcement: you may read and enjoy this book until you're blue in the face; you may even quote a paragraph or two in a review; you may not reproduce this book in any way, by any mechanical, photographic, and/or electronic means – that is the exclusive right of the publisher and me. You must arrange further use of Letterbox with us. You can go ahead, now.

Adkins, Jan.
  Letterbox: the art and history of letters.

  Bibliography: p. 48
  SUMMARY: Traces the history of letters and examines the evolution of different styles of calligraphy and printing.
  1. Lettering – History – Juvenile literature. [1. Lettering – History] I. Title
NK3600.A34   745.6'1'09   79-48050
ISBN 0-8027-6385-5   ISBN 0-8027-6386-3 (lib. bdg.)

12084

First published in the United States of America in 1981 by the Walker Publishing Company, Inc., and simultaneously in Canada by Beaverbooks, Limited, Don Mills, Ontario.

Trade ISBN: 0-8027-6385-5
Reinforced ISBN: 0-8027-6386-3

Library of Congress Catalog Card Number: 79-48050

Printed in the United States of America

10 9 8 7 6 5 4 3 2 1

STUVWXYZ

I am fascinated by letters. When I was in junior high school my art teacher, Eli Munas, taught me to letter with a pen and then a brush. I lettered signs, posters, doors, pool depths, cards, certificates, and never learned to paint from that talented man. The shape and flow of letters stay with me; they surface in my designs, my illustrations, and I could not write without the feeling of pen on paper. I covet new pens, I keep searching for the perfect nib and the discreet flourish that will wow the gas company into silence. I admire the look of big letters and think their shapes are among the seeds of shapes. With thanks to many people, including Kate's mum, Thea Adair, bravura penman Raphael Boguslav, foredefeated challenger of oblivion John Benson, and devisive designer Peter Kemble, I dedicate this book to friends who have the old shapes in their heads and hands:

Trina Schart Hyman
John Grandits
George Tilley

Vanity of vanities saith the preacher, all is vanity, what profit hath a man of all his labor which he taketh under the sun? One generation passeth away and another generation cometh, but the earth abideth forever, the sun also ariseth and the sun goeth down and haseth to the place where he arose, the wind goeth toward the south and turneth about unto the north, it whirleth about continually, and the wind returneth again according to his circuits, all the rivers run into the sea, yet the sea is not full, unto the place from whence the rivers come thither they return again. — ecclesiastes

People have always talked; you can't imagine a time when folks haven't sat over their meal and talked about the big things, little things, sweet things, and scary things they wanted to share. And later at night, around a fire, the stories! The close sound of voices is something people have always needed, but other needs came with changing lives. Families began keeping herds together, settlements of families stored grain together, villagers laid down property lines, city people agreed with their trade controls and disagreed with their armies. There were needs for cattle counts, grain and land records, treaties, demands, ultimata, troop orders, letters of surrender, and proclamations of victory. At some point people had to write, to send messages further than the loudest shout, beyond the hill.

Surely writing began simply, an effort to send some fact or feeling over a distance. At the beginning writing might have been a token: a flower left outside the flap of someone's tent must have sent a tender message. Earliest writing could be a warning, too: scouts ahead of a wandering tribe left marks in stones and branches to tell the others of direction, conditions, danger. Writing could be a special mark, made by one people or tribe or even by one man to say "this well was dug out by the people of the reed-place," "this bow was made by the hand of Chui the hunter." The marks that began writing had to be simple and well-shaped to be recognized over and over. Writing had to be an art, then, and there are few arts closer to people's doings than the art of the writer, because nations

A storyteller with a pictograph of a hunting journey.

and even ages strive through the writer's hand to communicate further than the next town or the furthest village; they shout through his fist across time. The lines of communication the writer stretches from place to place and time to time make a web in which we can catch the sense and shape of the wide world.

The earliest writing left for us to see comes from one of the earliest needs: to communicate the biggest, most important feelings and times, things that seem too big for words, things to be shared with everyone forever. We can still see the pictographs—picture stories—painted on cave walls that tell us very well about the great hunts and the great dangers and the wonderful, frightening power of a running bull. It is very good writing.

Pictographs tell simple stories: a man leaves his home and walks for six days through forests and over mountains; he and other men hunt wild cattle with a spear, he kills two, one man is hurt and carried away; he comes home by water, a journey of four days. The pictographs indicate these real events. They suggest facts, just as modern pictographs—road signs and automobile switches—suggest facts about the road ahead and what the switches control, but pictographs can do little more than show simple nouns. The "reader" must fill in the action. A storyteller could *say*, "How sweet home looked to the returning hunter," but he could not *write* it in pictures. And how could a picture say, "He had missed his wife and children," or "He loved the smells of his own valley." Happiness, loneliness, love, and smells can't be seen, can't be pictured.

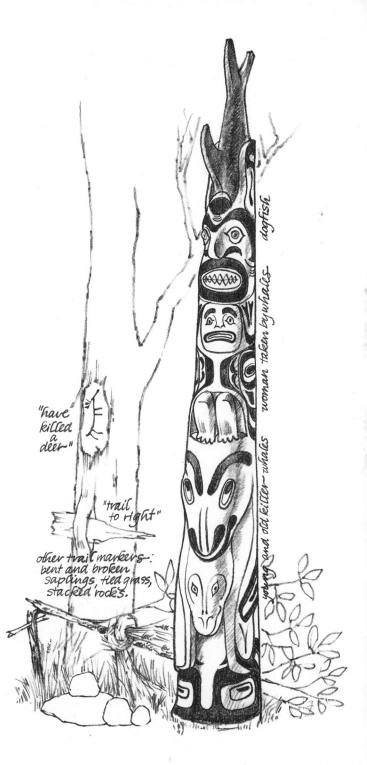

"have killed a deer"

"trail to right"

other trail markers: bent and broken saplings, tied grass, stacked rocks.

young and old killer-whales

woman taken by whales

dogfish

A universal symbol: the skull

A hobo symbol: Man with gun lives here

Nautical chart symbol: visible wreck

man   woman   child

family

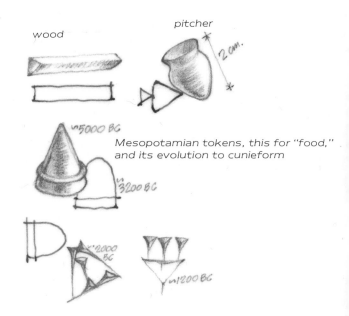

wood   pitcher

Mesopotamian tokens, this for "food," and its evolution to cunieform

Oneway to write feelings, smells, wishes, things that can't be seen, is to make a symbol that stands for them. In the hunting story a sun stands for *day*. A moon can represent a *month*. A bull represents *strength*, a turtle can symbolize *safety*. A snail can be *slowness*, a bird can be *swiftness*. What would be a symbol for warmth, for cold, for fragile, for wet?

Symbols combine to make new symbols. A mother and child can symbolize *love*, a hand and a hammer can say *work*. What would an eye and drops of water symbolize?

Symbols say something quickly and give information and warning in a clear way. Symbols are sometimes better than writing with letters, because people who speak different languages "read" many of the symbols that are all around us.

The difficulty of writing with symbols is plain: too many symbols. It would be an enormous task to learn a separate symbol for each thing, each action, each feeling, color, smell, belief. Japanese and Chinese *calligraphy* (writing) is symbolic, though, with more than fifteen thousand *characters* to represent everyday things and complex ideas. The oriental calligrapher works with brush and ink on paper, silk, bamboo strips, wood

8

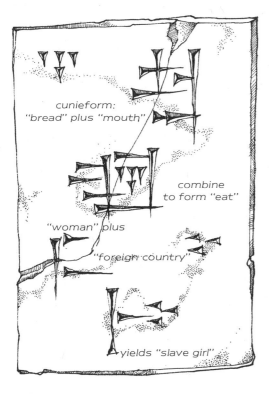

cuneiform:
"bread" plus "mouth"

combine
to form "eat"

"woman" plus

"foreign country"

yields "slave girl"

tree   forest

courage/valor

woman   son   love/goodness

Chinese weights and measures law recorded during the Chin Dynasty on bamboo strips

plaques. His skill is considered a great art. Chairman Mao Tse-tung relaxed with calligraphy and was proud of his work.

Writing tools shape writing. The characters made with brush and ink will have a flowing curve; symbols drawn with a reed pen are more precise. Some of the oldest writing was probably the work of tokens, tiny models shaped like bread loaves or wheat shocks or sheep, pressed into damp clay to keep trading records. The Mesopotamian *cunieform* was similar; a wedge-shaped tool (cunieform means "wedge-shaped") was pressed into clay to make distinct characters. The clay tablets were baked and sent out like hard postcards or stored as records. These imperishable tablets are our records of the day-by-day life in Sumeria, Assyria, and Babylonia four thousand years ago.

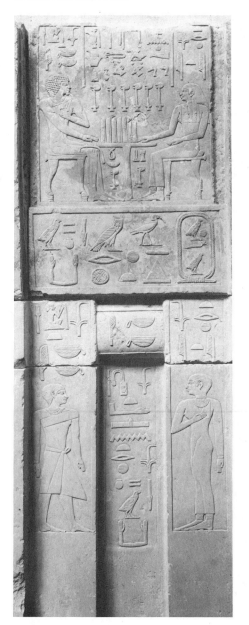

Egyptian writing began as a symbol system, but changed over thousands of years to include new forms. At its beginnings it must have been picture-writing, but it adopted symbols (sometimes called *ideograms*, "idea pictures") which were used with the pictures. Much later the formal writing of Egypt may have absorbed hundreds of *phonograms* ("sound pictures") which stood for syllables. In this way a word could be put together like a rebus puzzle. Still later Egyptian writing may have accepted an *alphabet* in which each symbol represented a sound, sounds making syllables, syllables building words. We think. The puzzle is that Egyptian formal writing suddenly appears fully formed in the inscriptions of the First Dynasty (a very early period of Egyptian history). Nor is there only one Egyptian *hand* (style of writing) to puzzle over, there are three: *hieroglyphic* (meaning "priestly pictures," the formal, decorative hand for official inscriptions), *hieratic* (meaning "of

the priests," a faster hand for less formal writing), and *demotic* (meaning "of the people," a simplified everyday hand for business and correspondence). In some inscriptions all the hands were used together in a confusing, complicated, beautiful tangle.

Thousands of years later the sprawling, ruined civilization of old Egypt was a stupendous puzzle. It was not a dark mystery without a shred of evidence. There was evidence everywhere: inscriptions, scrolls, bright paintings of hunts, feasts, and ceremonies. The people in the pictures were calling to the awed citizens of the new world but we were deaf. We could not read the old writing.

Then a young lieutenant in Napoleon's Egyptian campaign noticed a smooth black stone. Digging around it he discovered a basalt slab about as large as a kitchen chair, and about a foot thick. He brought the stone, carved with three inscriptions, to his general. One of the inscriptions was in hieroglyph, one in demotic, and one in Greek. Greek? Greek could be read easily! If all three inscriptions said the same thing, the Greek inscription could give keys to the hieroglyphs. It was not that simple. It was not simple at all: it took many years and it took Jean François Champollion.

At sixteen Jean could speak eight languages and when he applied to the college at Grenoble in 1807 he was accepted—not as a student but as a teacher. He studied constantly. He went hungry and wore ragged clothes through many winters, he survived revolutions and ruined his health to pursue the key to the old writing, but as smart and as curious as he was, the beautiful hand defied him for twenty-five years. He did not find it all at once—very few discoveries are made simply and quickly—but after a lifetime of work the old Egyptians pictured at the feasts and ceremonies and hunts spoke to him in their strange language of ideographs and phonographs and letters from the ancient world.

THE ROSETTA STONE

There are places and times we can never hear, cultures and people whose voices are too distant or too few to be understood. It is a great achievement of minds to hear even a few voices from long ago.

Do you wonder who will hear us a thousand, two thousand years from now? All our paper books and documents will be gone then. What will archaeologists read? If they can decipher them, a few inscriptions on buildings, many tombstones, aluminum roadsigns, Pepsi bottles, license plates, store names etched on glass, samplers stitched in linen. What will they think of us?

One culture that didn't care what the future would think of their writing was the nation of Phoenician traders. They were middlemen: they put cash down in Egypt, traded in Crete, and sold at Athens . . . all at a profit. Profit was their god and their goal. Egyptian thought looked toward the setting sun, toward the new world of gods that death would open; the Phoenicians got up early and plied their trade from sun to sun. They were here-and-now merchants. The graceful, decorative hand of Egypt wasn't fast enough or flexible enough to handle trade in a dozen languages. What was wanted aboard a Phoenician merchantman was a way to keep records, nothing more. Their hand was angular, quick, and purely alphabetic—one letter, one sound. They had no written vowels (like a, e, i, o, or u), though they must have spoken them. Their writing was a shorthand—thy wrt fw lttrs n gssd wht t sd ltr.

The Phoenicians were middlemen in a most important way: they bridged a gap between the formal, fixed thinking of the Egyptian dynasties and the free-flowing, abstract questioning of the Greek city states. The hand they passed on to the Greeks (where it changed even more) was suited to a language that was growing with new, unseeable concepts that pictographs could never show.

| L | K | J | TH | H | Z | F | H | D | G | B | glottal stop |

Phoenician letters

| W | T | SH | R | Q | TS | P | mute | KS | N | M |

When Greek characters were developed over centuries they included vowels, new characters, and some attractive curves. The same Greek is used today, not only in Greece, but in science and mathematics (two abstract studies the Greeks loved). Any freshman physicist can recite the list of Greek letters, which begins α (alpha), β (beta) . . . The Greeks passed their letters on to us, so it is quite right that their first two letters should give us a name for our letters: the alphabet.

A	B	G	D	Ē	DZ	H	TH	I	K	L	M
alpha	beta	gamma	delta	epsilon	zeta	eta	thēta	iota	kappa	lambda	mu

Greek "alpha-bet"

N	X	O	P	R	S	T	U	PH	KH	PS	O
nu	xi	omicron	pi	rho	sigma	tau	upsilon	phi	khi	psi	omega

13

Simple things change slowly, but everything changes. The *A, K, D,* and *M* we use are the most recent forms of characters that have been used every day for six thousand years and more. They are so much a part of people's lives that no one *plans* to change them; it just happens, and it is remarkable how few forms they have taken.

The Greek letters were straight and handsome, affected by the short, straight strokes necessary when writing with a *stylus* in a wax tablet. The hand had a regular, marching look. Older writing might be made bottom to top, right to left, left to right, or top to bottom. Early Greek *scribes* wrote left to right until the end of the line and then came back from right to left on the next line. They called this *boustrophedon*, meaning "ox-turning," like an ox ploughing a field, but the later Greeks decided on one way, and we've written left to right since then. ALL THE LETTERS WERE CAPITALS (small letters with capitals were not used until the tenth cen-

the cartouches, or royal seals, of King Ptolemy and queen Cleopatra, with their letter explanations and the signature, in Greek, of Cleopatra

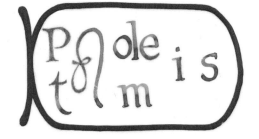

14

tury AD). There was no space between words (andyouknowhow difficultthatwouldbe), and there was no punctuation! Crazy? Yes, maybe it was; punctuation (including devices like parentheses—not to mention hyphens) is a great help.

hieratic

demotic

Greek

ΤΟΙΣΤΕΙΡΟ
ΙΣΚΑΙΕΓΧΩ

apis the bull hieroglyph	demotic	late demotic	early Greek	late Greek	Roman
apis the bull hieroglyph				A	A
kaph the palm				K	K
daleth the door					D
cheth the fence				H	H
water and the owl				M	M
lameth the whip					L

15

The Romans adopted and adjusted the Greek hand in the same confident way they adopted and adjusted the Greek gods. They did not take the alphabet entire and complete, but developed their own style and characters as the Greeks were still developing theirs, and the two styles diverged. Thirteen of the 21 Greek characters stand whole in the Roman alphabet, and the remaining letters are similar to Greek—they have a family resemblance.

It is rare in history to see one point, one pinnacle standing above others in the range of events, that becomes a landmark. History doesn't happen that way: attitudes change, favor shifts, styles change, governments grow weak or strong slowly, but landmarks are important and historians sometimes choose peaks and call them pinnacles, just for reference. The Roman emperor Trajan commanded in 106 AD that a column be erected commemorating his victories in the Dacian Wars; it was good politics. Roman calligraphy had been developed and refined for centuries as a major part of art and architecture — and politics. It was at its peak when the finest stonecutters in Emperor Trajan's Rome carved it into hard marble.

The beauty of our letters comes from the thousand-year work of scribes before the Trajan column, but those letters are so fine and noble that it is not unfair to say it comes from them. Those letters are delicate and strong at the same time, straight and curved, stern and lyric. It is impossible to say whether they are so beautiful because of their grace and function or because of our acquaintance with letters that came from their stock, but they are one of the benchmarks of craft and art. They are beautiful in themselves.

Trajan's Column

the Trajan Inscription, from the base of Trajan's Column in Rome; letters of such grace
and dignity that, together, they are a silent discourse on form and proportion

*(Photograph of an accurate replica of the inscription on the Trajan column in Rome, now on permanent exhibit at The Lakeside Press,
R. R. Donnelley & Sons Company, Chicago.)*

SEMPER PA
VPER ERIS
SI PAVPER E
S AEMILIAN

Writing is too important to life to be merely decorative. Writing works. Men and women make the decisions that change life, but writing carries their decisions, makes a record of them. Laws hold a society to its goals of fairness. To be successful the law must be the same for every person and every village, so it must be accurately reproduced in writing to "the letter of the law." Trade missions, armies, diplomatic legations must carry orders, send back reports, and receive new orders. In a great government the enormous number of decisions and details

the emperor Trajan

ISSA·EST·PASSE
RE·NEQVIOR·
CATVLLI·ISSA
EST·PVRIOR

cannot be made by one person or by a hundred; they are made by thousands of men in hundreds of bureaus, each bureau sending out requests, orders, reports, and keeping records *in writing*. Writing records the purchase of farms, the grinding of wheat, and the selling of bread.

So it was in Rome. The high beauty of carefully drawn Trajan capitals was an ideal, but it could not keep up with the scribe's workload. A quicker hand was needed—easy, readable, above all *standard*.

Capital letters are named

NUPER·ER
AT·MEDICU
S·NUNC·EST·
UISPILLO·DI

uncials

fepцima·ia
m·philerof·
цibi·condicu
r·uxor·in·a

half uncials

hnc·fefцmaca
requiccac·ero
qon·umbra·cn
imin·E·quam·
faci·fexcapc

informal·Roman handwriting

from their being carved on the *capitals*, or tops, of columns. Today we begin sentences, names, and place names with "capital" letters but in first-century Rome there were no *UPPER CASE* and *lower case* letters to make such distinctions. The Roman capitals were copied at first for all manuscripts in a style called *quadrata* (named for the square cut of the reed pen). Of course everyday writing—letters to friends, store accounts, notes—were written more rapidly and with less care, usually with a stub pen or with a stylus on wax tablets or lead

sheets. The formal hand followed the informal scrawl, and the quickness of the pen showed in the fourth-century *rustica* letters (*rustica* means "rural" or "countrified"), which are degenerate capitals. By the fifth century the formal hand had changed into an attractive new style which was more than a poorly written capital; the new letters were called *uncials* because they were usually done to about the height of a Roman inch, or *uncia*.

The uncials are simple and beautiful. They flow naturally and are easy to form. The reed

pen influenced the style. You can see this best if you make a reed pen for yourself.

Half uncials follow informal hands more closely. In writing quickly, the vertical strokes of letters were sometimes carried above or below the letter height to make certain letters more readable. These strokes are called *ascenders* and *descenders*, and you can see them in the half-uncial style.

The capitals, uncials, half-uncials, and everyday hands were the forms with which Rome communicated with its vast empire.

19

Alsyui pGi umtenitum Aeen mtutr nobir aditum

Merovingian

The Roman Empire did not fall, it faded. For reasons too varied and complex to know or to tell, the government in Rome weakened and could not support its wide territories and huge armies. The center would not hold and the edges of the Empire, the conquered territories secured by legions, collapsed inward. Over time the far regions, without firm direction from a central government, took control of their own affairs and centered management around a local warlord or strong town, In times of war citizens of local communities were obliged to serve their local lord; the lord, and lords of other communities, were pledged, in turn, to serve regional lords; they, in their turn, were servants of a king. This web of obligations is called *feudalism* and for seven centuries it served a Europe of isolated communities. Without the stream of direction, without news and new styles from Rome, local pockets of activity closed into their cocoons. This lack of communication is why the Middle Ages (ninth to sixteenth century, generally) are called the Dark Ages.

A strong king could exert great influence, especially with the help of the Church. Karl the Great, a French king also called Charlemagne, was a successful general and — most important — a talented administrator. Pope Leo III, in the weakened Rome of the eighth century, allied himself and the Church to this strongman of Europe by creating him Holy Roman Emperor. With this additional political power, Karl shaped the world around him, and one of his important influences was on writing.

The skill of a great administrator is to choose superior men and women for difficult tasks. Karl showed his skill by choosing a scholar from Britain, Alcuin of York, to organize a reform of the European hands.

Isolation had encouraged a decay of the standard Roman hands. The regional hands practiced by careless scribes were difficult to read, varied in form and spelling, and the documents and manuscripts they recorded were spread out across Europe in hundreds of monastery *scriptoria*. In 789 AD Karl the Great ordered that *all* law, literature, records, and church services be recopied in the hand that Alcuin had chosen as the most readable.

The scholar Alcuin had chosen and developed a plain, round hand used in France. He simplified certain characters and fixed writing practices. Further, he used punctuation, sentences, and paragraphs. Even though *majuscule* letters (upper case, or capitals) were not used with *miniscules* (lower case, or small letters), this hand is called *Carlovingian miniscule*, probably because the ascenders seem to mark the height of larger letters. All the characters are familiar to us today with the exception of the tall *S*, which was used well into the nineteenth century.

We owe the shape of our miniscules to Karl the Great and Alcuin of York, but we owe them more than that. Because they collected and recopied the manuscripts of Europe, they saved for us the laws and literature of Greece and Rome. They passed on to us the words of the ancient world. Karl could be proud as he signed his name to his momentous orders, but to the end of his life he remained illiterate—he made a diamond with a pen and his scribes added the rest.

Carlovingian miniscule

Mattheuſ · ſitque q quaternario denario numero triformiter poſito principium

BENEDICTUS

Carlovingian majuscule

21

It is not surprising that Carlovingian changed, because ideas were changing. In art and architecture the vertical shaft eclipsed the horizontal mass, the round Roman arch gave way to the pointed "Gothic" arch, the solid low walls necessary in Roman engineering were overshadowed by high, windowed walls which new construction advances made possible.

The round, plain quality of Carlovingian was lost in this shift to the vertical and the pointed. Following the shapes of new regional hands, writing of the twelfth to sixteenth century became more severe, darker, less flowing, and less readable.

This style is now called *Gothic*, but it is a name given as an insult by later Renaissance artists; they were rediscovering and reviving the "classic" styles of Rome and Greece and thought the styles of the Middle Ages were poor and even barbaric, in the manner of the barbaric Goths.

Early Gothic was precise and very angular. A whole page had the effect of a fabric-like texture and was called, accordingly, *textur*.

Later curves and almond-shaped rounds called *mandorla* were part of a style called *schwabacher*.

Fraktur was a combination of rounds and verticals, and was used into the twentieth century as a national newsprint type in Germany.

In these styles, made with reed pens and ink, scribes copied the books and records of their age. The Egyptian scribes had worked on *papyrus* scrolls, sheets made by pressing and drying a wet crosswork of beaten reeds. There was such a trade in papyrus reeds that Egypt stopped their export, and a substitute was found: the hide of a kid or sheep was split, pounded and polished to make a smooth, flexible sheet that took ink without fuzzing or beading. This writing surface is so durable that most of our earliest manuscripts are written on it. It was a major trade item from the city of Pergamom, and our name for it (changed from centuries of use) is *parchment*. The Chinese were the first to make paper, but their skills were learned by Arabs. The Arabs brought paper to Spain, and from there its use spread, so by the sixteenth century paper was available over Europe and ready to lend itself to a giant step in the history of writing.

textur ···· tight angular

abcdefghijklmnop
qrstuxyz

schwabacher ⸺ mandorla rounds

abcdefghijklmno
pqrstuxyz

fraktur ⸺⁘⸺ a combination

abcdefghijklmn
opqrstuxyz

23

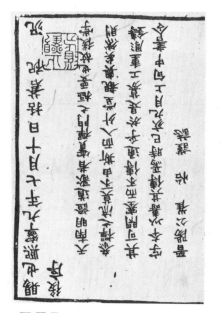

Gutenberg's Press

We call it "the Renaissance," the rebirth, and what we mean is that the stern attitudes of isolation and guilt that ordered the ideas of the "gothic" times had given way to new thoughts. A dark view of this world as the preparation for death lightened to a happier appreciation of earthly life. Stilted church decoration bowed to a new interest in a more natural art, especially in the sculpture of Greece and Rome admiring the bodies of men and women as the yardstick of beauty. The feeling of the Renaissance was a new "humanism"; it was a respect for an individual person's worth, for the effort and art a person could produce. In this climate of waking senses and budding ideas communication was more important. New readers demanded books and papers but letters were still shaped one by one, fingers plying reed pens. Books were still the result of many weeks' copying, treasures to be owned by the rich and powerful. Humanism needed a new medium to broadcast its ideas, and to this urgent need Johannes Gutenberg applies his excellent mind.

The curious thing about Gutenberg is that he did not take one timid step toward improving an art; he leaped forward to make a new art, entire and whole. He invented the tools, worked out the formulae, perfected the processes and — most astonishing — set standards in his earliest examples that are respected by his art today, five hundred years later.

Printing, even printing books, was not new in the fifteenth century. The Babylonians had "printed" impressions in wet clay with cylinder seals. The art of carving wood blocks, inking them, and transferring the pattern to parchment or paper was well-known. There are Chinese books printed in the eighth century and a system of printing with movable wooden type had been developed in Korea.

Gutenberg developed a method of casting an alphabet of characters in lead alloy, setting them into lines, inking them, and pressing paper onto the inked surface. Since he used a master mold for each character, his letters were identical, perfectly formed to make straight lines and clear impressions. His work was so thorough that he would be familiar with foundry type today, with letterpress methods and (mechanization excluded) equipment. He might note with pride that our printer's ink is made from the same ingredients he decided on and that our letterpress type is cast with a lead alloy mixed almost exactly to his formula.

Gutenberg's respect for the calligraphy of his day is evident in the style of type he cast, the work of his collaborator, scribe Peter Schoeffer. They tried to reproduce the best hand-lettering, the rhythm and precision of a gifted scribe, and succeeded. Other claims are made to the invention of printing, but Johannes Gensfleish zum Gutenberg von Mainz succeeded so well that we think of his accomplishment as the respected beginning of the humanist art of printing.

a page from the Gutenberg Bible (Used with permission of The Pierpont Morgan Library)

The Renaissance had spirit. In a flurry of invention and inquiry artist-engineers built machines, bridges, buildings; philosopher-courtiers examined the nature of

power, government, life; scholar-adventurers dug up art buried with Rome and Greece. Antiquity delighted the men and women of the rebirth; they found that the guiltless nudes, the earthy plays and poems and papers, the ordered practicality of the "classic" era were somehow closer to them than the grim-lipped saints of the dark "Gothic" ages. In their zeal to replace the old with the older, they made some "classic" mistakes.

The Gothic hand displeased them. They saw it as a remnant of a stifled age. New manuscripts were written in the hand of the ancients: the proud majuscules they found on Roman capitals and the miniscules they found in the classic manuscripts. But the manuscripts they cherished were not written in ancient Rome; they were copies of the Roman originals set down in Carlovingian miniscule by order of Karl the Great, a hand unused for hundreds of years. Their second mistake, calligraphically, was using majuscules and miniscules to-

humaniſtic miniſcule ~ 15th C.

No counſel iſ more truſtworthy than that which iſ given upon ſhipſ that are in peril ⁙

Leonardo da Vinci : 1452·1519

abcdefghijklmnopqrſtuvwxyz

gether. The two hands had never been meant to support each other; one was for stone inscriptions, one for parchment and reed pen. Nevertheless, there they are. We cannot fault them too much for choosing a wonderful miniscule and a wonderful majuscule because we write with them today.

Everyday hands acquired greater importance in the Renaissance. More people were writing. Communication was the current of the rebirth, running from one mind to another between cities and countries. The most beautiful and lasting hand in this humanist revolution is a *current* (running together, quick) *cursive* (slanted) brought to a peak by the Italian writing masters who published books of handwriting for students to copy in the sixteenth century. They called it *cancellaresca* and we, for its Italian origins, call it *italic*. It may be the most natural and beautiful handwriting ever practiced and we shall see it again in more than one form.

Angling was an employment for his idle time, which was not then idly spent: for angling was ... a rest to his mind, a cheerer of his spirits, a diverter of sadness, a calmer of unquiet thoughts, a moderator of passions & a procurer of contentedness ⚓ The Compleat Angler

a Renaissance italic hand by the author

portion of a letter written by Elizabeth I
in the italic hand (Copyright The British Library)

that you saye that I giue folkes occasion to thinke in refusinge the good to vpholde the iuel I am not of so simple vnderstandinge, nor I wolde that your grace shulde haue so iuel a opinion of me that I haue so litel respecte to my none honestie that I wolde maintene it if I had sonficiente promis of the same, and so your grace shal proue me whan it comes to the pointe. And thus I bid you farewel, desiringe god alwais to assiste you in al your affaires. Writen in hast. Frome Hatfelde this 21 of Februarye.

Your assured frende to my litel power. Elizabeth

27

Printing was so necessary, so desired, that in the 35 years after Gutenberg's Psalter of 1454 was printed, presses were operating throughout Europe. In 1458 Charles VII of France heard of Gutenberg's invention and, knowing only that the printing was done with metal type, he cleverly sent a "spy" who knew how to work metal.

Nicholas Jenson was a jeweler, a medalist, and director of the Royal Mint. His business was designing coins and medals, fashioning molds and tools to make them, and overseeing their production. No one was more qualified to make the next step in printing. He traveled to Mainz to learn the new secrets, but when he returned in 1461 the new king, Louis XI, had little interest in printing. The master of the mint resigned his position and, in 1469, he was set up in the printing center of Europe, Venice.

To this point, type had copied hand-lettering with minor variations to suit the limitations of printing mechanics. Jenson saw type as a new form with needs that were more than mechanical. Legibility and beauty were his standards, and copying a scribe's characters too closely would compromise both. He saw clearly that type was cut in metal, not written with a reed pen, and he designed a new *face* (a style of type) that kept the grace and proportions of the best scribe's work though using the advantages of the metalworker. He kept the serif as an aid to the eye in rapid reading, he kept the form of the Renaissance *humanist manuscript* hand, but it was subtly different. It was, in fact, the type we know today, as readable and workable for us as any face the last five hundred years has produced.

About thirty years after Jenson cut the upright type we call *roman*, another Venetian printer was cutting a face based on a different humanist model. Aldus Manutius had used printing in its ideal popular purpose: he had published a series of small, inexpensive books, classics of Greek literature, in a Greek face. To continue his work (and it was very profitable) he was preparing to publish a series of Roman classics in Latin. For this project he designed and cut, on the lines of an informal hand, a current-cursive face. The grace and flow of this face (as well as the series itself) was popular, and it remains today as *italic*, a name referring to Renaissance Italy, which passed on to us so much knowledge in such beautiful forms.

.FINIS.

H oc ego nicoleos gallus cognomine ienſon
Impreſſi:miræ quis neg& artis opus?
A t tibi dum legitur docili ſuetonius ore:
Artificis nomen fac rogo lector ames.

.M.CCCC.LXXI.

the colophon, or printer's inscription, at the end of one of Jenson's early works (By permission of the Houghton Library, Harvard University)

the colophon of an Aldine classic (By permission of the Houghton Library, Harvard University)

Impreſſo in Vinegia nelle caſe d'Aldo Romano,
nel anno . MDI . del meſe di Luglio, et tolto con
ſommiſſima diligenƶa dallo ſcritto di mano me
deſima del Poeta, hauuto da M. Piero Bembo
Con la conceſſione della Illuſtriſſima ſi
gnoria noſtra , che per . x . anni
neſſuno poſſa ſtampare il
Petrarcha ſotto le
pene, che in lei
ſi conten
gono.
✳

Naval General Order

The President of the United States believing that greater formality in the infliction of such corporal punishments as are authorized by Law may be adopted in the Navy with beneficial consequences, directs, that no such punishment shall be inflicted on any person in the service without sentence of a court martial, when that is required by Law, or the written order of the Captain or Commanding Officer of the vessel, or Commandant of the Navy Yard to which he is attached, where the authority to cause it to be inflicted rests in the discretion of the commanding officer, specifying the offence or offences, and the extent of the punishment to be inflicted; which order shall be read, and the punishment inflicted in presence of the Officers and Seamen belonging to the vessel or Navy Yard.

Navy Department
May 29th 1840

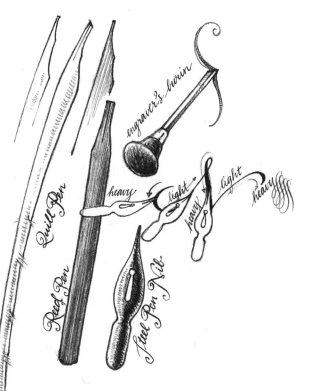

Printing did not diminish handwriting, but the scribe served different needs: those of commerce instead of culture. Commercial trade became the bulk of communication in the centuries after the Renaissance had awakened Europe. Though there were constant hostilities breaking into wars, the feudal web of military obligations was not nearly as effective as business for profit in weaving a net of communication across a much larger world. Profit charged that net with energy and urgency more intensely than feudal quarrels could have. Governments had their armies and navies, they fought and died, but victories of nations were being won with a catch of herring or a crop of wheat. Business correspondence flew in salvos between merchant-cities, scribes plied new pens with deadly precision.

Pens changed and styles with them. When the writing masters reproduced their copybooks, it was done with engravings, printing plates of copper incised (cut in) with sharp tools. These tools, *burins*, made a distinctive cut, a swelling curve that affected the character of the hands shown. Over time, pens became more pointed and more flexible to make that special engravers' curve. The square-cut reed gave way to the pointed quill and, eventually, to the pointed, flexible steel pen.

The *cancellaresca* developed in the Vatican chancery evolved into the *ronde* (developed in the French financial ministry) and then to commercial hands we recognize today as *scripts*. Writing masters' copybooks were dominated by order forms, forms of receipt, and inventory. A hand that found lasting service in commercial, governmental, and formal use is the *English roundhand*, a *commercial script*. It is a lyric, flowing hand, not especially readable but undeniably elegant.

Writing masters persisted in showing "proper penmanship" well into the late nineteenth century, but their work was less and less personal, and though it still has a few tired flourishes left over from the zany excesses of the baroque and "bravura" hands, it seems lifeless and cold. Where is the honest strength of the uncials, the upright order of Carlovingian, the poetic thicks and thins of *cancellaresca* in that last faded descendant of the writing masters, the Palmer Method?

an order from the British Admiralty to Lord Nelson (Reproduced by courtesy of the Trustees of the British Museum)

type

Art follows its age, follows the logic of its time. Styles come and go with the advance and decline of ideas. Nothing is separate from the stream of days; though a mode or a style or a whole discipline may sleep in an eddy for a time or run ahead in a surge of inventive current, everything moves. Nothing escapes the flow.

The change in typefaces is part of the history of ideas. The form of type reflects romantic periods, puritan austerity, the Industrial Age, classic revivals, severe functionalism, even disenchantment with a mechanized world. These influences are not exact or seen in entirety: that shaping of ideas can be "felt" more than seen, but an age surely guides an artist's hand.

Type can give more distinct impressions than the feeling of an age, that is why we have more than one type. Of the hundreds of *body* types (type for setting paragraphs such as this) with which a designer can have a book *set* (have the type set up in lines to print), each face has its own character. The designer tries to select a face to match the *copy* (the writing to be set). Some faces are somber, some are crisp, some are delicate, some are casual. There are typefaces so like another that the only difference is a slight variation of what a typographer calls *color* (the look of a whole page of one typeface). Some faces are so assertive that it seems ridiculous to set the wrong copy with them. Typography is a subtle art you may not have been aware of until this moment, but you have been seeing it work since you began to read. Now you know it is there, though, and from now on you will look at the character, the style, and the color of typefaces you see. You will be your own typographer.

. . . Holmes and I set off to Baskerville Hall, leaving the naturalist to return alone. Looking back we saw the figure moving slowly away over the broad moor, and behind him that black smudge on the silvered slope which showed where the man was lying who had come so horribly to his end.

Hound of the Baskervilles
in Baskerville

. . . All that most maddens and torments; all that stirs up the lees of things; all truth with malice in it; all that cracks the sinews and cakes the brain; all the subtle demonisms of life and thought; all evil, to crazy Ahab, were visibly personified and made practically assailable in Moby Dick.

Moby Dick in Zapf Book Medium

Early to rise and early to bed makes a male healthy and wealthy and dead.

James Thurber in Optima

In Xanadu did Kubla Khan
A stately pleasure dome
    decree:
Where Alph, the sacred river,
    ran
Through caverns measureless
    to man
Down to a sunless sea.

Kubla Khan in Tiffany Light

If a man does not keep pace with his companions, perhaps it is because he hears a different drummer. Let him step to the music which he hears, however measured or far away.

Thoreau in Helvetica

If liberty and equality, as is thought by some, are chiefly to be found in democracy, they will be best attained when all persons alike share in the government to the utmost.

Aristotle in Memphis

. . . And grey-eyed Athena sent them a favoring wind, a fresh blowing Zephyr, that sang over the wine-dark sea. And then Telemachus called to his comrades to look to the tackle and hoist sail . . . the bellying canvas filled, the ship flew through the deep blue water, and the foam hissed against her bows as she sped onward.

Odyssey in Futura

We catched fish and talked, and we took a swim now and then to keep off sleepiness. It was kind of solemn, drifting down the big, still river, laying on our backs looking up at the stars, and we didn't *ever* feel like talking loud, and it warn't often that we laughed—only a little kind of a low chuckle. We had mighty good weather as a general thing, and nothing ever happened to us at all.

Huckleberry Finn in Souvenir Light

There is nothing more difficult to take in hand, more perilous to conduct, or more uncertain in its success, than to take the lead in the introduction of a new order of things.

Machiavelli in Goudy Old Style

. . . To myself I seem to have been only like a boy playing on the seashore, and diverting myself in now and then finding a smoother pebble or a prettier shell than ordinary, whilst the great ocean of truth lay all undiscovered before me.

Sir Isaac Newton in Clarendon Light

. . . What a piece of work is a man! How noble in reason! how infinite in faculty! in form and moving how express and admirable! in action how like an angel! in apprehension how like a god!

Hamlet *in Weiss Italic*

TEENYBOPPER gadzooks!
HAMBURGER
WINDOW

THUD.
Disgusting.
SHAPE UP.
Forget it

Hellbox is the song and dance of type. Hellbox is how typographers refer to all the decorative types, the *display faces*. They are descendants of the large decorated initials on old manuscripts, pushed into fanciful shapes by the ballyhoo of advertising. Broadsides, large sheets of song or satire or political writing sold by printers and *chapmen* in the eighteenth century, had large type. We have hundreds of faces today, but the heyday of hellbox was the nineteenth century. Advertising in newspapers, circulars, and posters used a thousand faces cast in metal and carved in wood. Sign painters did up carts and wagons and lettered trade signs, foundrymen cast and woodworkers carved letters for storefronts, glaziers etched letters and curlicues into the windows and mirrors of saloons.

Display faces have emotion in them. They are perfect examples of art affecting emotion. They can wheedle and whine, shout like a calliope, strut, purr; they can be fat or old and shaky, straightforward or flip. They can say more than the words they spell. Listen, they say, listen to your eyes.

34

Whisper louder!

and fries

two cups rancid lambfat

CURDS & WHEY

BLACK
EYE

POPCORN

PEANUTS

ARSENiC

CRAWDADS

Christopher Latham Sholes

(Courtesy International Business Machines)

The death knell for beautiful handwriting was not sounded by a great blow but by a tiny, infernal tap-tap-tapping—the typewriter.

As business and bureaucracy grew, the volume of paperwork grew with it. Handwriting could be legible and even beautiful, but it was slow. In 1850 a contest for speedy scribes

was won with a rate of only 30 words a minute (a proficient typist today can easily produce 120 words a minute).

The typewriter is a fruit of the Industrial Revolution, but it sent out buds and shoots as early as 1714 when Queen Anne issued a patent to Henry Mills for a machine that "impressed letters singly or progressively, one after the other, as in writing." One of the first United States patents was issued by President Andrew Jackson's administration to William Burt for a "typographer" that fed paper through a roll much as a modern "typographer" does. In 1867 *Scientific American*'s July issue discussed John Pratt's printing machine—it was called the "Literary Piano"—but the direct ancestor of the modern machine appeared in 1868, the clever invention of a curious man.

Christopher Latham Sholes was a printer, a publisher and an Illinois state legislator. He was also a social reformer, a feminist advocating equal rights and votes for women, and a tinkerer. In Kleinstuber's Machine Shop he tinkered with the help of Kleinstuber's tools and his staff of German machinists. Before 1868 he had invented other devices leading to the typewriter: a machine for addressing newspapers and a printer for numbering theater tickets consecutively (not very different from the small ticket printers today). In 1873 he and his business partner, Charles Glidden, marketed the first typewriter manufactured for the public.

By the 1890s interest — and competition — in typewriters was keen. Designs were whimsical, practical, and monumental: the "Bennett" was two inches high and ten inches long with 84 characters, the "Bradford" had 300 characters including most common words, the "Megagraph" weighed 400 pounds and was six feet high. Advertisements were exuberant about the typewriter's effect: "no other machine, no other invention, no other article of commerce of any kind has ever played a more commanding role in the shaping of business and social destiny." Certainly the feminist Sholes would have approved the spirit if not the sincerity of Remington & Son's claims for women: "No invention has opened for women so broad and easy an avenue to profitable and suitable employment as the 'typewriter,' and it merits the careful consideration of all thoughtful and charitable persons interested in the subject of work for women."

What was the effect of the typewriter? Perhaps women did participate more broadly in business — if at a menial level. Certainly business correspondence moved faster, perhaps it was more legible. Mark Twain wrote his brother on his new machine, "It piles an awful stack of words on one page. It don't muss things or scatter ink blots around, of course it saves paper."

The typewriter is elegant in its delicate complexity, an admirable machine, but it is a machine. What it prints presents itself mechanically, dry and lifeless. Where is the *fist*, the human quaver, the soul that can flow onto a page quite outside the meaning of the words. Nothing two dimensional lives like the words written by a friend's hand. Reading through the arid files of typewriter tap-tap-tapping one longs for Mark Twain's lost inkblots.

Oddly enough Christopher Sholes loved letters, loved the printer's and calligrapher's art. Writing masters visiting Illinois always received free advertising in his newspaper.

In a few pages we have glanced at communication changing over six thousand years. What now? How will people communicate in the next century? If you could ask Julius Caesar that question, he might hope for better roads into Gaul and Africa. Jonathan Swift, who wrote *Gulliver's Travels*, would probably believe in better navigation and faster, safer ships carrying the word from one place to another. Benjamin Franklin, who started the postal service in the United States, might have a canny idea that electricity, one of his most curious riddles, would carry messages in the second century of the Union. Samuel F. B. Morse, whose telegraph and simple code sent messages across continents, surely foresaw messages free of the copper wire. Could Marconi, who freed the same code from the wires and sent it as a ripple through the earth's magnetic field, have foreseen communication satellites circling the earth, beaming down phone calls and

television news? What now?

In the immediate future we can easily see the great net of electronic communication growing denser and closer to every part of our lives. As almost every home now has a telephone (who would have been sure of that in 1930?), it is fairly certain that within the next fifty years every home will have a computer terminal that connects the household with stores, markets, libraries, schools, services, train stations, airlines, and entertainment companies all over the world. Every home will have access to stored information about history, medicine, home repairs, school records, congressional voting, recipes, stock market prices, road conditions, and even what is in the refrigerator and pantry! It will become possible to communicate quickly with anyone in the world as the size of radio receivers is shrunk by microcircuitry to wristwatch size. Business meetings will be carried on by conference telecast and most

business letters will be sent, received, and stored as electromagnetic impulses on the keyboards, display consoles, and storage tapes of linked computers. All this is today's certainty.

What is the next leap, the coming breakthrough in communication? A good guess might be ESP, extrasensory perception. It is provable that many people are adept at sending and receiving simple messages and patterns by some, as yet inexplicable, effort of concentration. If this process can be learned and amplified, communication will have overcome the barriers of time and place and weather that have kept people and nations apart.

Do you find this future of communication exciting? Do you also see the dangers and discomforts of a net of communication with a web so fine and pervasive as to strain the simplest and most necessary human needs? The dangers will be greater as communication becomes more widespread. With a telephone in each home we can reach out to the world. But we can also be reached, and it is difficult to ignore the urgent noise of a ringing telephone. What of videophones? They are well within reach, but do we want them? Telephones, televisions, computer nets, and instant, universal communication can break open our privacy. They can rob us of our aloneness, that dark and rich place where ideas and feelings develop and character grows. They can deny us self-reliance and weaken the warm ties of need that bind the family. Instead of grasping the support of brothers, sisters, parents, and friends, we could easily fall back on the impersonal press of the crowd, gabbling to us from every screen and receiver. What is the place of the alphabet, old and slow in its handformed beauty, in the flashing glow of the computer screen?

This IBM 6640 Document Printer, directed by a computer or by magnetic cards, can print up to 92 characters per second in a variety of typefaces, at any width, spacing, or size the operator selects. (Courtesy International Business Machines)

The Texas Instruments Silent 700, Model 765, one of the first of a generation of portable electronic data terminals. It weighs only 17 pounds and can fit under an airline seat. A newspaper reporter, a salesperson, or a researcher can plug it in anywhere and type copy, data, or information, which is stored in the 765's "bubble memory" (16–20 pages). The copy can be edited, changed, and added to. The 765 can then print a "hard" copy on paper or send its information to a base computer by telephone in a brief burst of condensed communication. Is this one of the ways we will conduct business in the near future? Almost certainly. (Courtesy Texas Instruments)

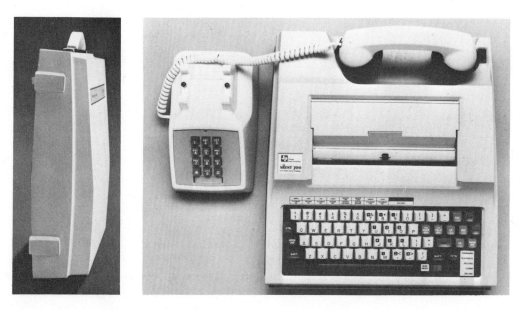

We are all in the business of communication. The only way we can live is to communicate accurately and persuasively: we ask for eggs, sign our names, calculate problems, show progress, describe difficulties, request help, order supplies, give directions, offer gratitude. We make our voices heard in sounds or letters in the most effective way we can.

Like sea creatures, we live in an ocean of communication, surrounded by information and opinion. To add our own thought to it, we must speak above the sound of the waves. How can a single voice compete with the rivers of words cascading into that sea from television, magazines, newspapers, and books? A high-speed printer can lay down 1,600 *characters* per minute (letters, punctuation, spaces); what can a person write or say in a minute? In this babble of machine chatter, what can be heard?

The sound of a friend's voice is so special that it cuts through the babble. We are humans and our ears are pretuned to vibrate to the familiar timbre of the human voice more than to all the clangs and clicks of machines quivering for our attention. We will always need the voices of children and friends and storytellers and we will always hear them, love them for their human beauty. What is the most beautiful voice you know? Is it perfect, like the humming of a dial tone or the toot of a pitch pipe? Or does it have its own quavers and rasps, familiar and welcome? To be heard in a world of machinery you must speak up clearly in your own special voice.

This is the place of letters and lettering. Like the sound of a human voice the written hand is imperfect, real, living. A letter from friend to friend takes with it meaning and comfort and information no other form of communication can carry. A letter written in your hand is unique. A letter may surprise you but it can never invade you; you will not be called out of your shower and forced to read it; you can read it when and where you want — in the garden, on the bus, in the bath. A letter is lasting: you can read it over and again, seeing subtle and unnoticed meanings on the second and third readings. A letter is a record: you can see a friend's attitudes change through his letters, feel her life change. Nobody ever bound up telephone calls in boxes to read years later, and Lincoln's telephone call to Mrs. Bixby would mean very little to us today.

For the writer a letter is more than a one-sided conversation in print. It needs your concentration and your best tongue to send its message. It needs clarity, structure, and sense. A letter is an opportunity to speak slowly and well, to communicate in the best way you can. The feel of pen on paper, the small world of the page, the feeling of accomplishment, the little thrill of dropping an envelope into the letterbox, and the anticipation of returning mail are some of the pleasures of the letter writer, the *correspondent*.

facsimile copied by author from original at Oxford College, Oxford

41

A short introduction to the Italic Hand

thick

3°-15°

thin

45°

the constant angle of the nib shapes the thicks & thins

If your first index joint is bent in your grip is too tight.

a d g

Write with a moderate slant and a light grip, the square nib at an angle of 45° to the line——

For the characters a, d & g there is a flattening of the tops and a sharper returning curve, like the tops of b, h, m, n.

abcdeffgghijklmnopqrssttuvvww'xyyzz & es

I have a strong hope that the letters we have seen in these pages will encourage you to shape your own. Lettering, *calligraphy*, is a simple skill that can be learned in a short time, practiced in everything you do, and perfected over a lifetime. You can get started in good style for two dollars and astound your friends, butcher, teacher, bank teller, and your own correspondents within a week.

The handwriting most of us learn is a variation on the steel pen roundhand, which, as you remember, developed almost mistakenly in copying the swells and loops made by engraver's tools. Without its thicks and thins, without its flourishes and expansive scale, roundhand is rather drab. If we return to the root of roundhand, however, we

Begin with an eye to ease more than accuracy. Accustom yourself to the form and shape of the letters, the feel of the nib and the proportions of the lines. Regularity and simplicity, which comprise the beauty of italic, are only accomplished with familiarity and without strain. When you feel confident in the basics you will have plenty of time to refine your technique. Some of the ligatures, or connections, possible are: st, ff, et, ft, tt, tt. The normal connections that bind the letters of a word into a whole can be learned with practice and are often wholly absent in a formal hand. Use and ease and your own input make a hand beautiful.

A ABCDE FGGH HI JKLMNOPQRSΓTUVWXYZ

find the humanist cursive, written with the square-nibbed pen, patterned on *cancellaresca*. Called the *italic hand*, it has the essence of good calligraphy—simplicity and clarity.

Learning the italic hand is largely a matter of avoiding complication. You will learn to keep the nib at the same angle, to write at an even slant, and to make simple lines and plain curves. The nib and the already familiar shapes of the letters will take care of everything else. Later you can add plumes and drum rolls, if you have the inclination, but you may find that forming the old, stark shapes that go back so far give the calligrapher a taste for the austere.

Clip the nib back at 90° to width; if you are beginning it is help- ful to practice with a broader nib, almost 1/16"

You can begin with an inexpensive cartridge fountain pen or you can soak an old fountain pen in lukewarm water and soap or a little ammonia to loosen old ink. Work slowly and carefully.

On a fairly fine stone or emery paper bevel the nib from the top, sharpening it like a chisel, keeping light and equal pressure. Use water or saliva as a stone lubricant.

Round the blade edge on an Arkansas stone or crocus cloth. Round the corners carefully and not too much. "Write" very lightly with the nib on crocus cloth or stone or on a brass sheet with jeweller's rouge. Examine the nib with a good lens; you can often see the source of scratching or rough writing — an unevenness in nib halves or a sharp bevel at one corner.

PAPER HELD SO NIB ASSUMES 45° ANGLE WITH LINES

a left-hand nib and paper position.

A word about writing tools: just as the flexible steel nib and the italic nib each write with their own character, other tools have their individual characters. The pencil, the felt-tip, even the ball-point, have special graces. Most calligraphers despise the ball-point and say it has killed good handwriting. To some extent they are correct. The ball-point is a terrible learning tool. The pen, felt-tip, and pencil are responsive to paper, pressure and angle, but the ball-point pro- duces a thin line without varia- tion and without feedback from the paper. A good calligrapher can write well with a ball-point, using its particular virtues of uni- formity and precision, but only after first learning the feel and flow of a pen.

When you have learned to

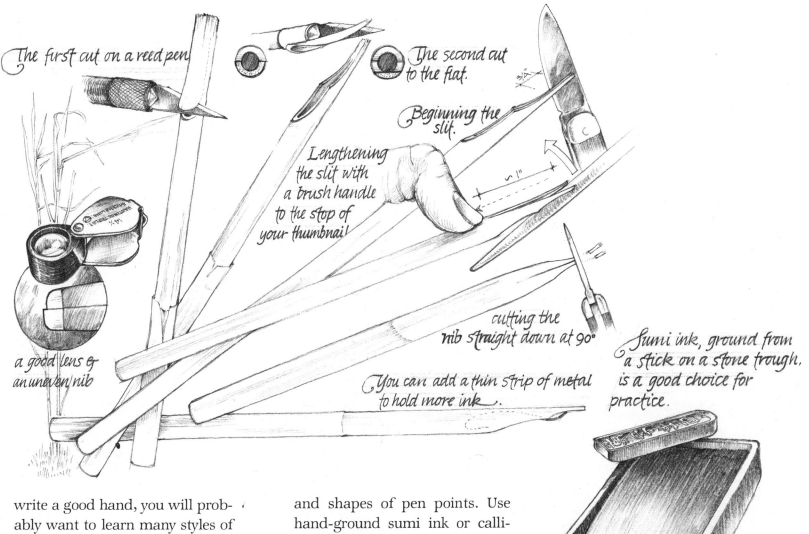

The first cut on a reed pen

The second cut to the flat.

Beginning the slit.

Lengthening the slit with a brush handle to the stop of your thumbnail

a good lens & an uneven nib

cutting the nib straight down at 90°

You can add a thin strip of metal to hold more ink.

Sumi ink, ground from a stick on a stone trough, is a good choice for practice.

write a good hand, you will probably want to learn many styles of lettering. You will begin to letter cards, posters, signs, axe handles, oar blades, doors, book covers, and chair backs. Cut yourself a reed pen and begin with simple, lower-case letters. Buy a few sizes and shapes of pen points. Use hand-ground sumi ink or calligraphic ink or dilute india ink. Try papers and colors and flourishes. In the bibliography of this book there are excellent lettering guides and several books to help you perfect your italic hand.

the magazine for children

logo for Cricket magazine by the author; a clockface by Raphael Bogus-lav; an alphabet stone by the John Stevens Shop, Newport, R.I.

Letters begin to murmur to you when you start to understand them. Their shapes are old and strong and burnished to spare elegance by much use. You will begin to hear them everywhere, to criticize this label or that sign, to be gratified by a well-turned G or a proud A. Your conversation with letters will become more fluent and happier. It is an old dialogue that brings out of you the artist, the craftsman, and the storyteller.

46

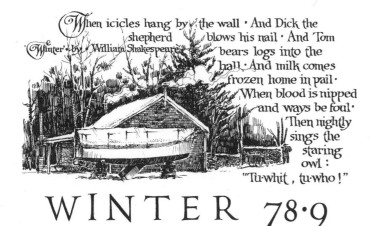

When icicles hang by the wall · And Dick the shepherd blows his nail · And Tom bears logs into the hall · And milk comes frozen home in pail · When blood is nipped and ways be foul · Then nightly sings the staring owl : "Tu·whit , tu·who !"

·Winter·by·William·Shakespeare·

WINTER 78·9

a card by the author; an architectural plaque by the John Stevens Shop; an italic alphabet with flourishes by Raphael Boguslav

MOSES MASON HOUSE
1813
Restored 1972–1973 in memory of
WILLIAM BINGHAM
& Presented by his Trustees to The
BETHEL HISTORICAL SOCIETY

47

I hope you will look into these books; they will excite and expand your appreciation of letters and calligraphy.

ABC of Lettering and Printing Types, Erik Lindegren, Pentalic, 1976
A Book of Scripts, Alfred Fairbank, Faber, 1977
Calligraphy, Arthur Baker, Dover, 1973
Calligraphy, Byron J. Macdonald, Pentalic
Calligraphy Today, Heather Child, Pentalic, 1976
Handbook of Pictorial Symbols, Rudolph Modley, Dover, 1976
Manuale Typographicum, Hermann Zapf, MIT Press, 1970
Lettering, Hermann Degering, Pentalic, 1965
Speedball Textbook, George F. Ross, Landau, 1973
Symbols, Sign & Signets, Ernst Lehner, Dover, 1950
Symbol Sourcebook, Henry Dreyfuss, McGraw-Hill, 1972
The Alphabet and Elements of Lettering, Frederick W. Goudy, Dover, 1922
The Art of Written Forms, Donald M. Anderson, Holt, Rinehart & Winston, 1969
The History and Technique of Lettering, Alexander Nesbitt, Dover, 1950
The Irene Wellington Copy Book, Pentalic, 1977
The Italic Way to Beautiful Writing, Fred Eager, Collier-Macmillan, 1974
The New Better Handwriting, George L. Thomson, Pentalic, 1977

The following institutions and corporations have been most helpful in offering suggestions and materials and granting permissions:

Raphael Boguslav
British Library, London, pp. 24, 27
British Museum, London, Courtesy of the Trustees, pp. 11, 31
Fogg Art Museum, Cambridge
Houghton Library, Harvard University, Cambridge, p. 29, top and bottom
IBM Corporation, p. 36, top p. 39
John Stevens Shop, Newport, R.i. p. 46
Liaison Office of the People's Republic of China
Museum of Fine Arts, Boston, p. 10, 14
National Archives, Washington, D.C., p. 30
Open Court Publishing Co., LaSalle, Illinois, p. 46
Oxford College, Oxford, p. 41
Pentalic Corporation
Pierpont Morgan Library, p. 25
R.R. Donnelley & Sons Company, Chicago, p. 17
Smithsonian Institution, Washington, D.C.
Texas Instruments, bottom p. 39